CAN YOU SEE WHAT I S
CHRISTMAS

READ - AND - SEEK

WALTER WICK

Cartwheel ·B·O·O·K·S·® SCHOLASTIC INC.

New York Toronto London Auckland Sydney
Mexico City New Delhi Hong Kong Buenos Aires

Text copyright © 2008 by Walter Wick.
All images from *Can You See What I See? The Night Before Christmas*
© 2005 by Walter Wick. Published by Scholastic Inc.

Library of Congress Cataloging-in-Publication Data
Wick, Walter.
Can you see what I see? : Christmas read-and-seek / Walter Wick.
p. cm.
ISBN 0-545-07887-3
1. Picture puzzles–Juvenile literature. 2. Santa Claus–Juvenile literature. 3. Christmas–Juvenile literature. I. Title.
GV1507.P47W5117 2008

793.73–dc22

2008001583

ISBN-13: 978-0-545-07887-0
ISBN-10: 0-545-07887-3

Printed in the U.S.A. • First printing, October 2008

Dear Reader,

Read the words and find the hidden objects. For
an extra challenge, cover the picture clues at the
bottom of each page with your hand.

Have fun!

Walter Wick

Can you see

a basket,

a chick,

and 2 bears?

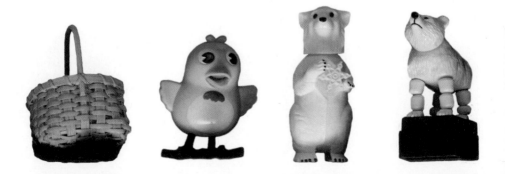

Can you see

a dog,

a pig,

and 2 chairs?

Can you see

a horse,

a snowman,

a moon?

Can you see

a ring,

a sled,

and a spoon?

Can you see

a clock,

a bear,

and a mouse?

Can you see

a horn,

a bear,

and a house?

Can you see

a cow,

a bell,

a red hat?

Can you see

3 birds,

a dancer,

and a cat?

Can you see

a bike,

a drum,

and a clock?

Can you see

a button,

a spool,

and a sock?

Can you see

a cone,

a fork,

and a train?

Can you see

a donkey,

a girl,

and a plane?

basket

bear

bell

bike

bird

button

cat

 chair

chick

clock

clock

cone

cow

dancer

dog

donkey

drum

fork

girl

hat

horn

horse

house

moon

mouse

pig

plane

ring

sled

snowman

sock

spool

spoon

train